ALL THINGS ELEPHANTS FOR KIDS

FILLED WITH PLENTY OF FACTS, PHOTOS, AND FUN TO LEARN ALL ABOUT ELEPHANTS

ANIMAL READS

WWW.ANIMALREADS.COM

THIS BOOK
BELONGS TO...

_____

_____

CONTENTS

WELCOME TO THE WORLD OF ELEPHANTS!

Do you hear that?

Listen well.

It sounds like a trumpet being blown loudly from afar! A trumpet from the largest living land animal in the world! **AN ELEPHANT!**

Elephants are one of the most awe-inspiring and fascinating animals on earth. With their mighty size and unique features, they are known as symbols of immense strength and overwhelming power. In many cultures, elephants are revered as cultural, religious, and spiritual symbols too. In the Far East, they have historically carried royalty on their backs, and even today, they represent wisdom, protection, strength, and good fortune. That's why you'll find magnificent elephant statues in certain parts of the world.

The mystical, impressive, and imposing elephant is also an incredibly gentle and nurturing creature. It is fiercely intelligent, resourceful, and a true force of nature.

Are you curious to learn all there is to know about the largest land animal on earth?

We bet you are!

So why don't you pack your bags and come along as we flip through the pages of this wild safari of a book... **let's go meet the formidable elephant!**

HOW DO ELEPHANTS TALK TO EACH OTHER?

They use their ele-phones!

WHAT IS AN ELEPHANT?

Elephants are indeed the largest land animals in the world today. In case you're curious, the largest animal in the whole world is the blue whale, but elephants are pretty gigantic as well.

The elephant is from the family **Elephantidae**, but unfortunately, almost all animals under this family are now **extinct**.

What does *extinct* mean? It means there is not even a single member of the animal species left on earth. Pretty sad, right? But it's not uncommon, to be honest. For one reason or another, many animals have gone extinct in the past.

Today, although it is accepted that species do go extinct from time to time, there are many organizations that help species that are **endangered.** As the term suggests, these are species whose numbers are so low that they are "in danger" of going extinct. Nowadays, experts, scientists, and conservationists do everything they can to help species survive.

Currently, there are only three known species of elephant left on earth:

- The African Savannah elephant
- The African Forest elephant

- The Asian Forest elephant

It's interesting to know that the two African elephant species are genetically different. This means their **DNA** is totally different – *that, basically, they are made of different building blocks.* The funny thing is that scientists only discovered this in the year 2000. Before then, even they thought the elephants in Africa were all the same!

Isn't it crazy how scientists make new discoveries all the time? It's marvelous!

So... where were we...right...ELEPHANTS!

Of course, all three species of elephants are closely related (*because with those long trunks and floppy ears, they really couldn't be anything **but** elephants*). Yet, they do differ in a few important ways.

Want to find out what they are?

Then c'mon, flip the page already!

HOW TO RECOGNIZE DIFFERENT ELEPHANT SPECIES

African savannah elephants are the biggest of their kind, while the African forest, and Asian forest, are similarly sized. The savannah *ellies* are also famous for living in very large family groups. Out in the open plains of Africa, they commonly live in groups that number 7-20 and even 80 members. The forest species, on the other hand – both in Africa and Asia – tend to live in much smaller family groups.

Can you guess why that would be?

Researchers have determined that environment plays a huge role in this curious difference. The savannah, being so big and open, makes it easier for very big groups to hang out together. In densely packed forests, however, it's very hard to keep large groups of animals together.

If you were an elephant, you'd be losing cousins and aunties at every corner behind tress and whatnot! So, to make life simpler, the forest elephants created much smaller groups. *It kinda makes sense, don't you think?*

Anywho, this also accounts for the size difference, according to experts. Those big, wide-open spaces are why the savannah elephant can grow up to **twice the size** of its forest-dwelling cousins.

FUN FACT: Elephants can grow up to around 10 feet tall and weigh up to 6 tons! Male elephants only reach their maximum size when they turn 35 to 40 years old. Even at birth, calves are already very large and can weigh up to 260 pounds!

The differences between the African and Asian species go back millions of years. In fact, scientists determined that these two species actually evolved from different ancestors.

But there'll be more time later to delve into the history of this extraordinary creature.

For now, let's get to know them a little better!

Elephants are **mammals**, just like us humans. This means they don't lay eggs but give **birth to live young** who **drink their mother's milk**. Female elephants are called cows, while male elephants are called bulls. *Sound familiar?!*

Elephants are also **herbivores** which means that they *only* eat plants. Cows, buffalo, elk, rabbits, chipmunks, and squirrels are some examples of herbivores like the mighty elephants.

This is an animal that loves to live in groups – even the forest elephant, which lives in smaller groups, is a very sociable animal.

For this reason, elephants have evolved a very complex system of communication. They 'talk' to one another in a variety of ways. They can use their trunk and blow it like a trumpet, touch or emit a scent, or even through body language. They can also cleverly communicate by using seismic signals meaning thumping the ground to create vibrations. Other elephants then detect this kind of communication through their feet bines.

Isn't that just mind-blowing?!

There are many aspects of elephants that make them truly unique animals. Most of all, their fascinating history.

Let's dive into their history, and we'll discover how and when they got to be so big when everything else didn't!

WHAT ANIMAL IS ALWAYS **UP** FOR AN ADVE**NTU**RE?

ELEPHANTS!

They have a trunk with them wherever they go.

HISTORY OF THE ELEPHANT

There are a few animals living today that look like they used to roam our planet millions of years ago, and one of them is the elephant. Something this large looks like it belongs in the dinosaur era, wouldn't you say? So, it's puzzling to know that all those massive animals that once roamed our planet have since gone extinct, whereas the elephant did not.

It also begs the question: did our modern-day elephant evolve from an even BIGGER animal in ancient times?!

Let's go ahead and find out!

Elephants are the only members of the **Proboscidean** family left on earth. This term (pronounced *pro-bo-see-deean*) represents 'animals with trunks.' In fact, the scientific name for an elephant's trunk is a *proboscis*.

FUN FACT: Proboscidea is a Greek word that means 'having a nose.' In the strictest technical term, that means humans are also proboscidean!

Once upon a time, this family of very large animals included all the elephants' closest relatives, such as the **mammoth** and the **mastodon**.

Scientists believe that the largest land animal that *ever* lived on our planet was probably a proboscidean.

And who are we to argue?

Proboscideans originated in Africa about 56 million years ago, which we're sure you'll agree was a very, very long time ago. Here they remained for well over 33 million years until one day, seemingly out of the blue, the elephant got a little bit curious.

After all that time living blissfully happy in the wilderness of Africa, elephants began walking in just about every direction. And walk they did. All the way to Europe and Asia, in fact! About 16 million years ago, they finally also arrived in the Americas.

That's quite the overland trip!

Fast-forward millions and millions of years, and all we are left with are three species of elephants living on only two continents: Africa and Asia.

Over the course of a very long time, elephants on all other continents went extinct. Scientists don't know *exactly* why the elephant's ancestors went extinct everywhere except Africa and Asia, but they have made two guesses.

Woolly Mammoths sadly all went extinct.

Firstly, they are pretty sure that all mammoths and mastodons were hunted to extinction by ancient humans. Then, the few that survived probably fell victim to the warming of the planet. Global climate change is nothing new, of course, and this has caused the demise of many species over millions of years.

THE ELEPHANT'S JOURNEY THROUGH EVOLUTION

To better understand elephants today, it helps to know more about their earliest ancestors.

Experts believe all elephants except the three species that exist today went extinct about 10,000 years ago. In the big scheme of things, that isn't very long ago at all.

Originally, all elephant-like species originated from an animal known as the **Palaeomastodon** that roamed our planet about 36 million years ago. This hefty dude lived in marshy swamps and was as comfortable in water as he was on land. Scientists believe that the trunk acted like a snorkel back then and helped trunked animals to breathe when they were swimming.

Now *that's* pretty awesome.

Over millennia (*that means thousands and thousands of years!*), the Paleomastodon evolved into the **mammoth**, which in turn became the African and Asian elephants we have today.

Can you name a famous mammoth? We bet you can! Manny from the Ice Age movies is a mammoth. And yes, the mammoths are the direct ancestors of the Asian and African elephants that live on our planet today!

LET'S TALK ABOUT THE MAMMOTHS

We can't possibly move on with our journey with the elephants if we don't talk about their ancestors, the mammoths.

Mammoths were characterized by their long and curved tusks, and contrary to popular belief that they were super-duper large, they actually weren't. Mammoths were about as large as modern-day elephants.

Perhaps the most famous of all mammoth species was the wooly mammoth. A species that lived in the northern part of the world and adapted to the colder and harsher environments by growing a long, thick, and brown wool coat.

In case you are wondering: yes, Manny from the Ice Age movies is a wooly mammoth! Were they as gentle as how they were portrayed in the movies? We can't really say for sure, but if they were ancestors of elephants, then maybe they were gentle giants too.

Wooly mammoths lived on our planet during the second half of the Ice Age, and unfortunately, they probably could not cope with warming temperatures, given they evolved to thrive in such cold, harsh climates.

It is amazing to know that nature lives in a very delicate balance on our planet. Even just one degree rise in temperature can have devastating effects on many animal species, both on land and at sea. This is why it's important that all of us do our best to protect our environment and prevent further warming of the planet.

Together, we can prevent more species from going extinct!

DO ELEPHANTS HAVE A CLOSE RELATIVE LIVING TODAY?

Are you ready for more surprises?

We are!

There are several species on earth today that are considered close relatives of elephants.

The most famous species closely related to elephants are **manatees** and **dugongs**, also known as sea-cows. Both of these animals had ancestors that moved from living on land to swimming in the sea, and that's something they share with the elephants. Except they, of course, have remained in the water all this time.

Manatees live in the Atlantic Ocean. There are species in West Africa and in the Americas, specifically in the Amazon Rainforest and all along the Florida coastlines. Dugongs, on the other hand, prefer to live in warmer tropical waters, so they are found in the Pacific and Indian Oceans. Dugongs are spotted in the Red Sea and all over the Pacific islands, as well as Australia. Dugongs are also herbivores and can grow up to 10 feet long. Not only that, but dugongs also live very long lives till around 70 years of age.

ELEPHANTS ARE
MY SPIRIT ANIMALS!

WHERE DO ELEPHANTS LIVE?

We now know that elephants used to live all over the world, and now they only live in certain parts of Africa and in Asia. But, what environments do they love to live in, and why do they have the pesky habit of traveling far and wide from time to time?

Let's find out!

THE HABITAT OF ELEPHANTS

African savannah elephants live in the wide-open plains of southern Africa. The savannah is an incredibly huge ecosystem made up of tropical grasslands; a region that receives an immense amount of rain during the summer. The savannah is unique because it has many short bushes but lacks trees, which means the sunshine can penetrate to the ground all over. Savannahs are regions that lie in-between tropical rainforests and deserts, so Africa is not the only place you will find them. Savannahs are also found in South America, Australia, India, and Thailand. However, there's *one* thing that makes the African savannah so very unique: **elephants live there!**

African forest elephants, on the other hand, live in thick wooded forests and rainforests in central and western Africa. Because they are much harder to find, these elephants are not as researched as their savannah counterparts. Moreover, as forests continue to be cut down in Africa, their habitat is becoming threatened, and they too, as a consequence, are becoming endangered.

Asian forest elephants, like their African forest cousins, also love to live in luscious forests where they use tree cover for safety. Their range in Asia is quite wide as they can be seen in about 13 Asian countries, including India, Indonesia, Vietnam, Cambodia, and China. Thailand is also famously home to around 4000 elephants, half of them living in captivity.

Experts like to separate the different elephants in Asia by subspecies, which is determined by their location. This is why you'll often see them called Sumatran elephants (after the Indonesian island) or Chinese elephants, and even the Sri Lankan elephants. They are not different species of elephants, but they have evolved a little over time simply because they have lived in slightly different environments.

So, are all elephants thriving in their own environment?

Perhaps unsurprisingly, elephants are having a hard time, both in Africa and Asia.

You see, elephants need a lot of room to live happily, as you can imagine. They are, after all, the largest animal on land! Yet their preferred habitats are threatened by human habitation in both their native continents, which means elephants are competing for food and land with us humans.

As a consequence, African Savannah elephants are considered endangered, and all forest elephants are now critically endangered. This is just one step before extinction.

In India, elephants are highly protected even though the country is home to almost 1.4 billion people and has very little spare room. Nevertheless, the Indian elephants are under a Wildlife Protection Act, and although they used to roam the massive sub-continent at will, they are now confined to 29 reserves.

The great news is that the world has realized these humongous gentle beasts need to be protected even more. There's a host of organizations

whose aim it is to preserve the lineage of elephants in Africa and Asia, and great efforts are
being made to increase the numbers of these
large mammals in the wild.

UNDERSTANDING THE RELATIONSHIP BETWEEN HUMANS AND ELEPHANTS

If you've ever been lucky enough to visit Thailand, you will probably have come face to face
with a beautiful Asian forest elephant. The
country has had a long love affair with the animals. So much so that over half of their elephant

population is actually domesticated. This means that almost 2,000 elephants live in camps and work with people.

In India, the situation is even more alarming. Today, the country boasts about 27,000 elephants in total, 3,000 of which are domesticated and living in camps. Just a decade ago, the wild forests of India were home to one million elephants.

So, what's the relationship been between humans and elephants throughout the years?

The first thing you should know is that elephants would NOT make good pets. Ever. Not only for the protection of people (elephants may seem gentle, but they are powerful, fierce, and unpredictable) but also for the protection of the elephant. These are animals that belong in the wild and, as such, deserve a life of freedom.

The relationship between humans and elephants goes back a long time and has been very complicated through the ages. Humans and elephants are known to have evolved at the same time in Africa. In ancient times, humans hunted the giant beasts for food and ivory, the material that makes up the tusks and teeth of elephants. Yet somewhere along the way, humans realized that there was a certain connection with the animal, one that could be exploited.

It was about 200 years ago that humans first began taming elephants. They were used in wars and treated as 'colossal living tanks.' The animals can barge through anything and carry enormous weights on their backs. Around this time, people also got a taste for sport hunting. Back then, Americans and Europeans used to travel to India and Africa solely to hunt elephants as trophies.

Ironically, these very hunters alerted the world that elephant numbers were dramatically decreasing. It is ironic because it would be the early hunters who would eventually become the loudest voices for elephant conservation.

The most famous hunter-turned-protector of elephants was US President Theodore Roosevelt. His story perfectly explains humans' relationship with elephants (and all other wildlife) through the years.

President Roosevelt was a very dedicated hunter, and he often traveled to Africa to hunt all sorts of amazing animals, including elephants. At the same time, because he did love wildlife so much, he set up the Forest Service in the US and collected countless pieces for the Smithsonian Museum of Natural History.

It wouldn't be long before elephants started to appear in children's books, films, and circus shows the world over. Although wildly exploited for years, elephant research and the awareness of their incredible traits have led to a worldwide drive to protect them at all costs.

Elephants, as we now understand them, are intelligent and caring. They have a complex system of communication among their families and have shown to have a good memory and problem-solving skills.

They are truly amazing creatures that have as much right to live on this planet as we do!

WHY DO ELEPHANTS NEVER GET HOT AND BOTHERED?

They always have their ear conditioning on!

UNIQUE CHARACTERISTICS AND APPEARANCE OF ELEPHANTS

The large trunk, the long tusks, the massive bodies, and the thick skin: what are the uses of all the elephants' unique characteristics?

Let's dig a little deeper and find out!

TRUNK

The trunk of an elephant is actually an extension of its upper lip and nose. The trunk is a muscle that is flexible and can be used for many tasks. An elephant uses its tusk the same way you and I use our hands...to grab stuff!

If you look closely at an elephant tusk, you'll notice that there's a growth that looks very much like a finger right at the tip. There are two of these growths in African elephants and one in Asian elephants.

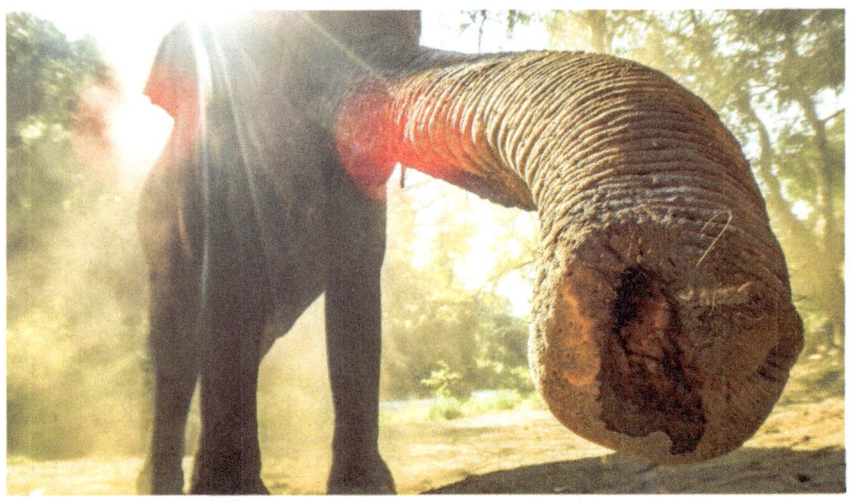

FUN FACT: There are quite a few animals that have trunk-like protrusions on their faces: from elephant seals to wild boar, antelopes, tapirs, and even anteaters have long 'noses' they use to grab stuff!

Of course, elephants also use their trunks for drinking from watering holes and rivers. **Did you know that an adult elephant's trunk can hold up to 2.5 gallons of water?!** And if you've seen an elephant documentary or two, you will also know that elephants can hold all that water in their trunks and shower themselves when it's too hot. Now that's what you call *super-cool*!

Elephants also use their trunks to take dust baths. This helps protect them from biting insects and the sun's harmful rays. **Like a dusty sun cream!** Unlike us humans, however, elephants do *not* sneeze when they inhale a large amount of dust into their noses.

Elephants are so good at using their trunks that they are famous for taking a peanut, shelling it, throwing the shell away, and then eating the peanut. All in one swift move!

They can also still use their trunks for snorkeling, meaning they can swim in the water while breathing easily by lifting their trunks high above it for air. Pretty smart, right? We think so too!

But that's not all: elephants even use their trunks to defend themselves from attackers. One swing of their trunk, and you'll certainly be in a lot of pain, even if you are a mighty lion.

Lastly (and what we love most), elephants use their trunks to greet and caress their fellow elephants or young. Seeing an elephant trunk embrace is pretty sweet indeed!

EARS

Animals in the wild don't have access to shelters like you and me, so they rely on their body to keep them cool or warm. An elephant's large ears help them stay cool, and the size of their ears depends on where they live.

Generally, African Savannah elephants have much larger ears than elephants living in forests. That's because they live in wide open plains, so they're exposed to a lot of harsh sun rays. Forest elephants in Africa and Asia, on the other hand, don't need to worry too much about sunstroke because they are protected by the forests' tree canopy, so their ears are much smaller.

Moreover, elephants have big bodies, so they produce a lot of heat. Since they cannot sweat like most animals, they need big ears to help keep them cool.

Apart from using their ears like a fan to cool themselves, this is also where excess heat escapes their bodies through blood vessels.

TUSKS

Tusks are none-other than an elephant's massive teeth growing out of their mouths! As you now know, they are made of a material called ivory, and they are incredibly important for the animals' survival.

An elephant's tusk will grow continuously throughout its life, extending deep within its upper jaw. A fully-grown tusk can weigh 100 pounds! These teeth are what's known as incisors, and guess what? **We have them too!** Luckily though, our own incisors never grow so big that they start sticking out of our mouths!

Elephants use their tusks for many tasks, including digging for water or minerals in the ground, lifting objects, gathering food, stripping the bark off their favorite delicious trees, self-defense, and protecting their trunks.

And if they ever need to fight, elephants also use their tusks to win a mighty battle!

FUN FACT: Much like humans usually have a favorite hand, they use more than the other (*is yours the right or the left?*) elephants also have a favorite tusk (*called the dominant tusk*) which they will tend to use more than the other! How do we even know this? Because scientists realized that all elephants had one tusk that was more 'worn out' than the other and eventually concluded that they also have a dominant trait.

SKIN

Did you know that our skin is the largest organ in our body? It is! So can you imagine just how large elephant skin must be?! Just as with us, elephant skin protects them from all outside threats.

Elephants have dark gray-colored skin that sometimes appears brown because they do love their mud baths, and mud tends to stick on their skin really well. If we never had baths after a mud fest, we'd probably look quite brown too!

The thickness of an elephant's skin varies throughout their body. It can be 1.5 inches thick in some parts and a little thinner in others. But, as thick as their skins can get, elephants are pretty sensitive, and they can feel even the slightest bite from an insect. That's why they do what they can to protect themselves from them.

African elephants have more wrinkles on their skin as opposed to Asian elephants, while the latter can have pink or light brown spots because they lack **pigmentation.**

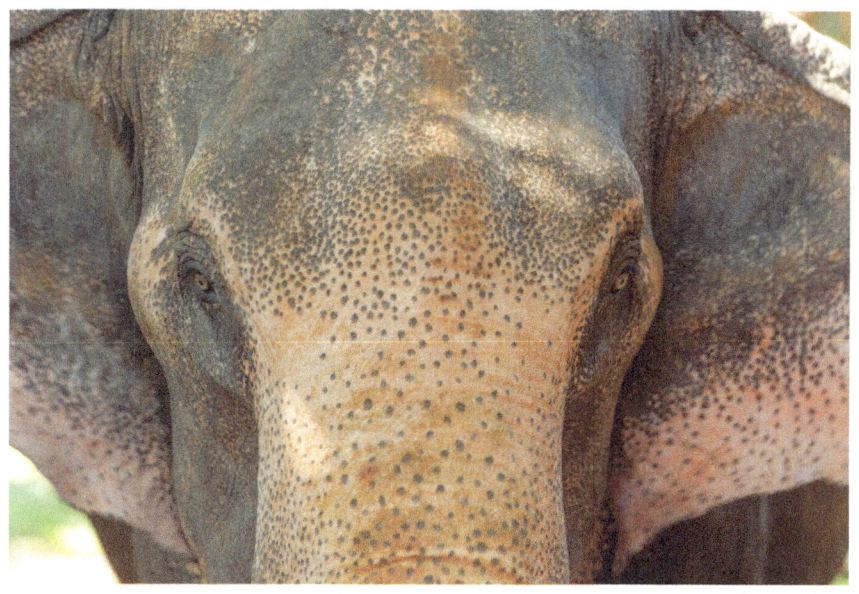

NOTE: Pigmentation means coloring. Some elephants can have a skin disorder where they lack the right amount of color in their skin.

So, why do elephants have cracks and wrinkles on their skin? Well, like their ears, those cracks and wrinkles also help them cool off. This is why African elephants who live in extreme temperatures have more of them compared to their Asian counterparts, who seem to be much smoother.

Such unique body parts these elephants have, right? We think so too! Let's move on to another important aspect of these large mammals.

What do elephants eat to grow so big and strong? Let's find out!

WHAT DO YOU CALL AN ELEPHANT THAT NEVER TAKES A BATH?

A smelly-phant!

WHAT DO ELEPHANTS LOVE TO EAT?

We now know that elephants are herbivores, but what kind of plants do they like to chow down on? And do they have favorites, like you and I?

Elephants can eat up to 375 pounds of vegetation in a single day! That's like two full-grown average-sized men. Yikes! Don't you worry, though, because elephants don't eat humans, and they only love to chow down on plants.

How can they manage to eat such a large amount of food? Well, to begin with, **elephants spend around 80% of their time in the day**

eating! That's about 18 hours just feeding and feeding and feeding themselves.

They also don't seem to be very picky with their vegetables (*unlike someone probably reading this book right now!*), and they will eat *almost anything.* They eat grass, bushes, small plants, twigs, fruits, roots, and even tree bark.

When it comes to water, elephants consume around 18 to 26 gallons on average but may drink up to 40 gallons in a day if they want to.

Sounds a bit too much, right? Well, know that adult male elephants can drink a whopping 55 gallons of water in just five minutes!

Elephants also dig the earth for salt and other vital minerals, as we mentioned earlier. This is how they add some more nutrients into their diet. Such amazing creatures, right? Even their diet and eating habits are fascinating!

WHAT DID THE MOMMA ELEPHANT SAY TO HER KID WHEN HE WAS MISBEHAVING?

"Tusk, tusk!"

LIFE CYCLE OF ELEPHANTS

Mama elephants (cows) are pregnant for about 22 months before they give birth to their single baby, called a calf. This pregnancy is more than twice as long as that of humans!

Humans are known to give birth to twins (or even more babies) more frequently than elephants. In fact, it's pretty rare for a cow to give birth to multiple babies at a time.

Unlike many other animals (like rabbits, cats, or dogs), elephants go through a very long pregnancy every four to nine years only, and, 99% of the time, they give birth to just a single baby.

This is one of the many reasons elephants have quickly become endangered.

Calves are born weighing around 260 pounds and are able to see just an hour after being born. They can also smell and walk if they want to. Within a couple of hours, they start drinking milk from their mamas. After merely two days, a newborn elephant calf can keep up with its moving herd. Calves rely on the milk of their mom for three months. Amazingly, they don't only drink milk from their biological mama but also from other female elephants from their herd!

Calves will continue to nurse (drink mum's milk) until they are around four years old, yet they start foraging the ground at around four months old. That is, once they learn how to use their trunks properly!

Males (bulls) are known to stay with their herd until they turn 10 to 12 years old, while cows stay with their herd for life. This is when they start becoming young adult elephants just right past their adolescence.

Elephants are considered fully grown once they reach 14 years of age. Elephants do live very long lives, and so they have a lot of chances to produce more babies. An elephant may live for 70 years. That's about the life expectancy of us humans.

Elephants also have a second chance at growth once they reach around 22 years old. That means that they will grow a lot bigger!

FUN FACT: As it turns out, the old tale of the elephant with the excellent memory really is true. Ellies in the wild usually have to memorize the identity of over 1,000 fellow elephants – leaders of the families (*the females*) spend their lives learning and remembering their family, friends, and enemies. This is why their memories have to become stronger with time. Their brains, by the way, are the largest of any land mammal (and weigh about three pounds!)

YOU'RE

ELEPHANTASTIC!

THANK YOU FOR READING!

We hope you have enjoyed learning all about the fascinating elephant, and if your love for this incredible creature is strong, you may want to learn more about efforts to protect them in the wild.

Elephants may be the largest and strongest land animals on earth, but sometimes, it's the ones who seem the strongest that need the most help.

The number of elephants in the wild are decreasing dramatically in both Africa and Asia, despite efforts over the last two decades to help protect them. If you are also concerned, here are some things you can do:

Adopt an elephant: The David Sheldrick Wildlife Trust is based in Nairobi, Africa. This incredible organization rescues and rehabilitates orphaned elephants and gives them a chance at a good life. You can foster a baby ellie to help them in their mission, and in return, you will receive photos and regular updates about how they're doing! (LINK)

Hold an Elephant FUNdraiser: Get your friends together and bake cookies, create elephant-themed cards for sale, or anything else you can think of to raise funds for an elephant protection group of your choice.

Start Planning a Safari With Your Family: When you visit a protected nature reserve known for hosting elephants, your entry fee will go back into protection efforts to keep them safe.

Share the Elephant LOVE with all YOUR Loved Ones: Sharing the love is half the battle won! Share all the amazing facts you have learned about elephants with your family and friends. Maybe they too will get involved in animal conservation, just like you. The mighty elephant needs all the friends it can get!

THANKS A TON!

THANK YOU!

Thank you for reading this book and for allowing us to share our love for elephants with you!

If you've enjoyed this book, please let us know by leaving a rating and a bricf review wherever you made your purchase! This helps us spread the word to other readers!

Thank you for your time, and have an awesome day!

For more information, please visit:

www.animalreads.com

ALL BIG **THINGS,**
START SMALL!

ISBN: 978-3-96772-097-6

ISBN: 978-3-96772-098-3

Animal Reads at www.animalreads.com

Published by Admore Publishing: Roßbachstraße, Berlin, Germany

www.admorepublishing.com

Made in the USA
Las Vegas, NV
15 December 2023

82911586R00046